ESSENTIAL FOREIGN INSULTS

This edition published 2012

First published in 2003 with text by Emma Burgess
Reprinted 2003, 2004, 2005, 2006, 2008 and 2010

This edition copyright © Summersdale Publishers Ltd, 2012

Summersdale Publishers Ltd
46 West Street
Chichester
West Sussex
PO19 1RP
UK

www.summersdale.com

Printed and bound in Great Britain

ISBN: 978 1 84953 275 4

Substantial discounts on bulk quantities of Summersdale books are available to corporations, professional associations and other organisations. For details telephone Summersdale Publishers on (+44-1243-771107), fax (+44-1243-786300) or email (nicky@summersdale.com).

CONTENTS

INTRODUCTION

Welcome, bienvenue, wilkommen (and various other insincere foreign platitudes) to Essential Foreign Insults!

We all love a holiday – the sun, the sand, the sea, and the opportunity to tell a member of the indigenous population where to stick their metaphorical, er, stick. With this little lifesaver of a book you are afforded the opportunity to confound locals far and wide with a barrage of colourful and offensive foreign guff. But be warned – if you're going to go toe-to-toe with a native in a slanging match, be sure to keep them at a distance; they do tend to whiff a bit.

Throw out the sun cream and start slapping on the insults!

GENERIC

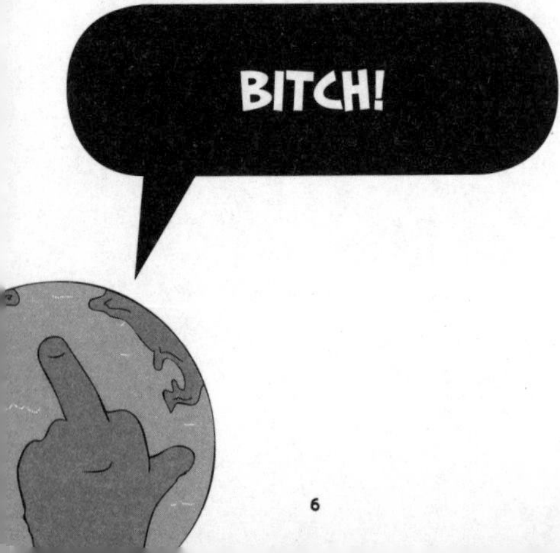
BITCH!

FRENCH
Salope!

GERMAN
Zicke!

ITALIAN
Stronza!

SPANISH
¡Zorra!

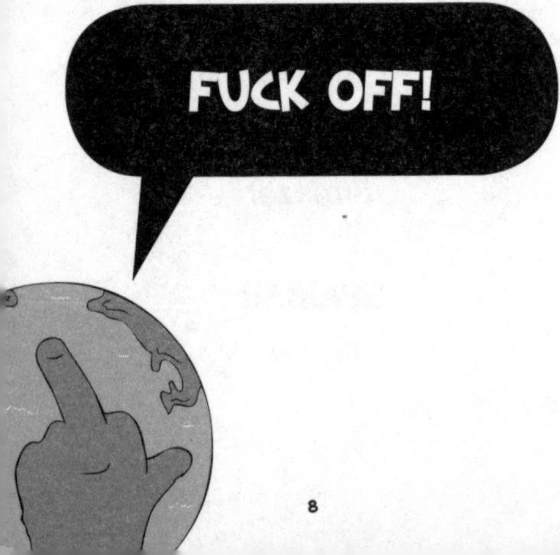
FUCK OFF!

FRENCH
Va te faire foutre!

GERMAN
Verpiss dich!

ITALIAN
Vaffanculo!

SPANISH
¡Vete a tomar por culo!

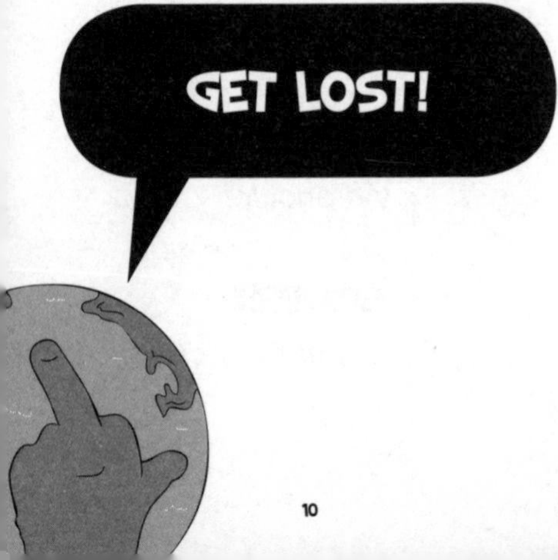
GET LOST!

FRENCH
Dégage!

GERMAN
Hau ab!

ITALIAN
Sparisci!

SPANISH
¡Pierdete!

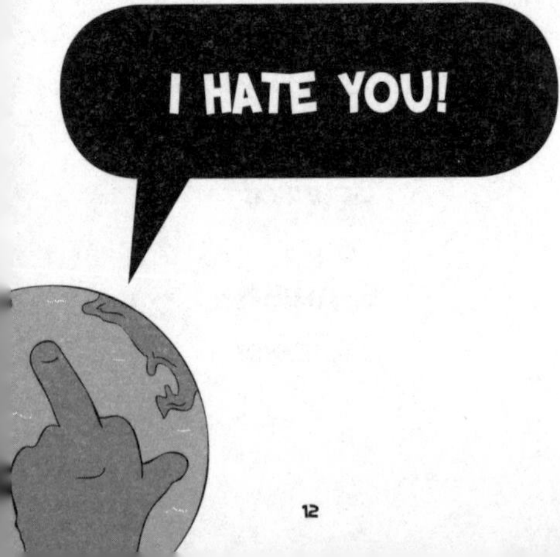
I HATE YOU!

FRENCH
Je te déteste!

GERMAN
Ich hasse dich!

ITALIAN
Ti odio!

SPANISH
¡Te odio!

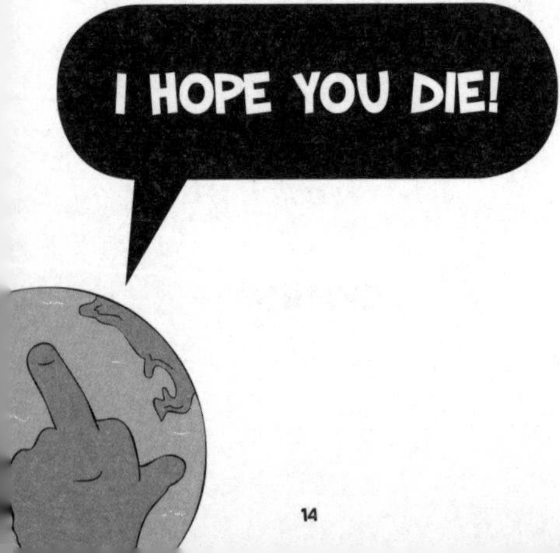
I HOPE YOU DIE!

FRENCH

Va crever!

GERMAN

*Tue uns ein Gefallen
und stirb schon!*

ITALIAN

Crepa!

SPANISH

¡Espero que te mueras!

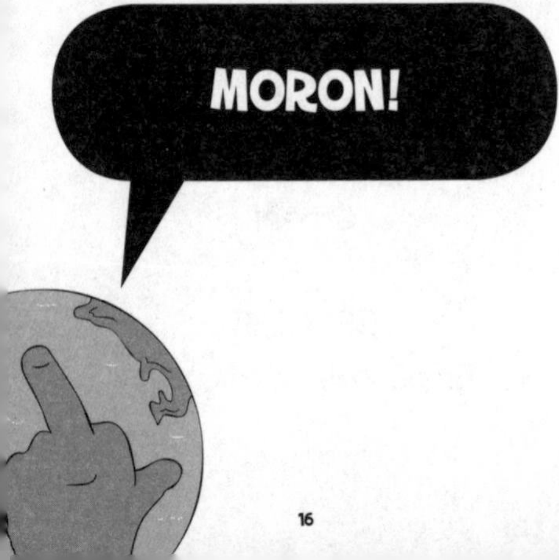
MORON!

FRENCH
Abruti!

GERMAN
Trottel!

ITALIAN
Cretino!

SPANISH
¡Retrasado mental!

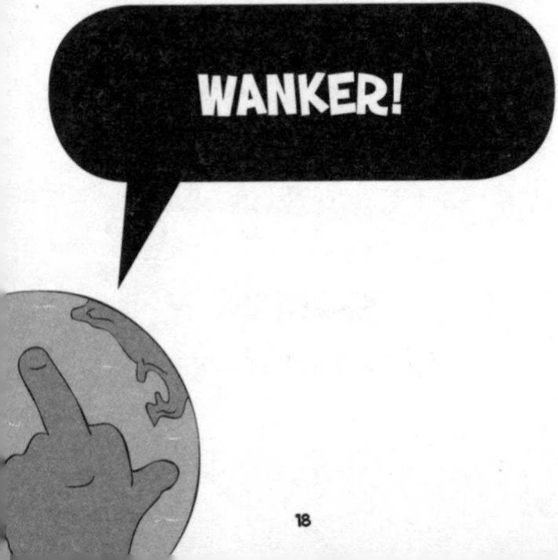
WANKER!

FRENCH
Branleur!

GERMAN
Wichser!

ITALIAN
Mezza sega!

SPANISH
¡Gilipollas!

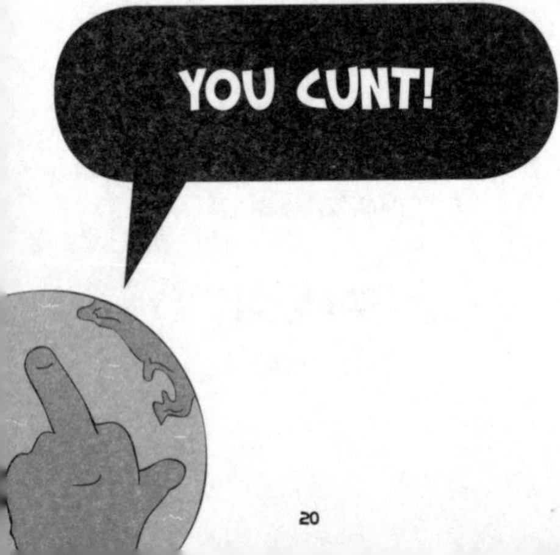
YOU CUNT!

FRENCH
Salaud!

GERMAN
Fotze!

ITALIAN
Fottuto!

SPANISH
¡Coño!

INVENTIVE

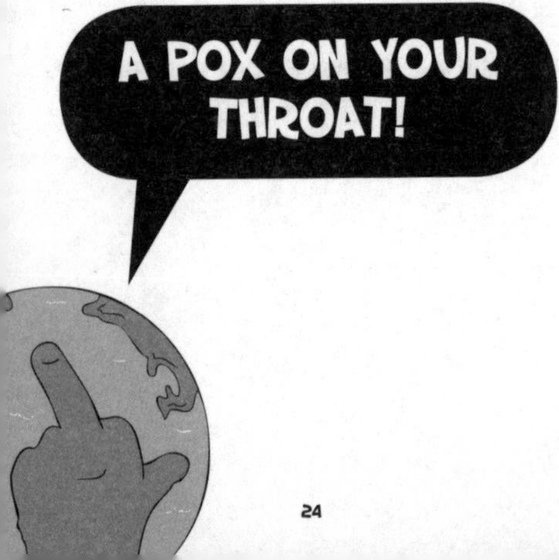
A POX ON YOUR THROAT!

FRENCH

Véreux!

GERMAN

Die Pest an deinen Hals !

ITALIAN

Ti colga la peste!

SPANISH

*¡Como un pincho en
tu garganta!*

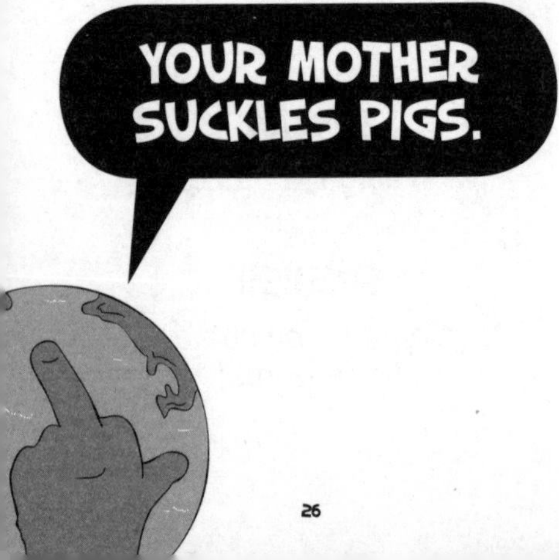
YOUR MOTHER SUCKLES PIGS.

FRENCH

Ta mère allaite des porcs.

GERMAN

Deine Mutter säugt Schweine.

ITALIAN

Tua madre allatta i maiali.

SPANISH

*Tu madre da de
mamar a cerdos.*

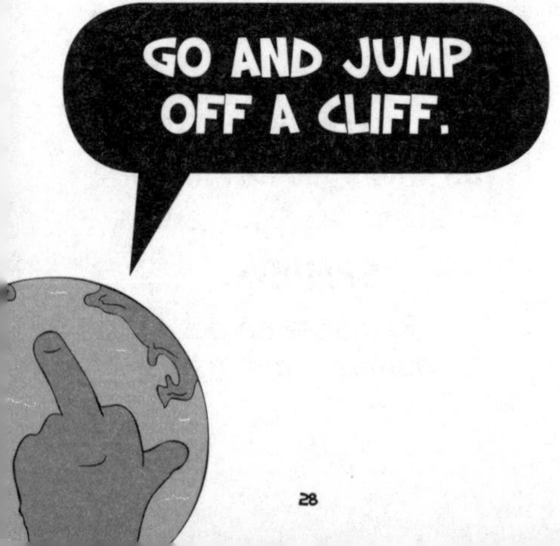
GO AND JUMP OFF A CLIFF.

FRENCH

Va sauter d'une falaise.

GERMAN

*Geh und stürz dich
von einer Klippe.*

ITALIAN

Vai e buttati da una scogliera.

SPANISH

Ve y tírate por un precipicio.

FRENCH

Ta mère était un hamster, et ton père sentait de baies de sureau.

GERMAN

Deine Mutter war ein Hamster und dein Vater roch nach Holunderbeeren.

ITALIAN

Tua madre era un criceto e tuo padre puzzava di bacche di sambuco.

SPANISH

Tu madre era un hámster y tu padre olía a bayas de saúco.

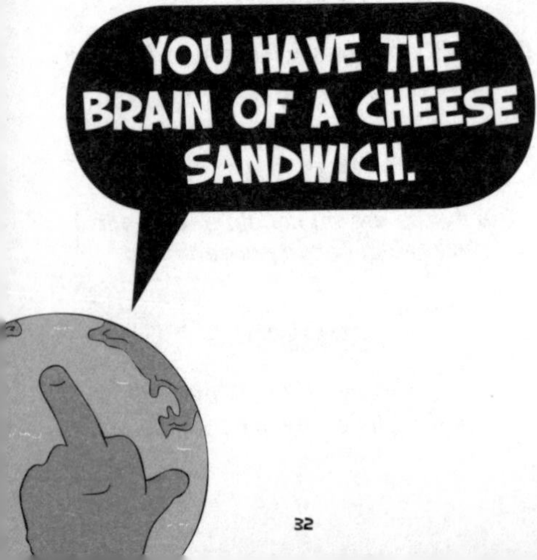
YOU HAVE THE BRAIN OF A CHEESE SANDWICH.

FRENCH

Tu as le cerveau d'un sandwich au fromage.

GERMAN

Du hast das Hirn eines Käsebrötchens.

ITALIAN

Hai il cervello di un panino al formaggio.

SPANISH

Tienes el cerebro de un bocadillo del queso.

100%
XENOPHOBIC

FRENCH

*Comme colonie de lèpre,
ton pays n'est pas mal.*

GERMAN

*Für eine Leprakolonie ist dein
Land ziemlich schön .*

ITALIAN

*Per una colonia di lebbrosi, il tuo
paese è abbastanza piacevole.*

SPANISH

*Como colonia leprosa, tu
país está muy bien.*

FRENCH

C'est fascinant, je n'ai jamais un pays avec autant de paysans. Oh, désolé! Je ne savaias pas que c'est ta famille royale.

GERMAN

Fascinierend, Ich habe nie ein Land mit so viel Proletariat gesehen. Oh, entschuldigung, ich habe nicht erkannt dass sie eure Königlich Familie seien.

ITALIAN

Interessante. Non ho mai visto un paese con così tanti contadini. O scusa, non sapevo che si trattasse della famiglia reale.

SPANISH

¡Que fascinante! Nunca he visto un país con tantos catetos. ¡Perdón! No sabía que fueran la Familia Real.

FRENCH

Ils sont tous aussi repoussants comme vous dans ce pays-ci?

GERMAN

Sind alle Leute in diesem Land so eklig wie du?

ITALIAN

Ma fanno tutti schifo come te in questo paese?

SPANISH

¿Es toda la gente en tu país tan asquerosa como tú?

IF THIS COUNTRY WERE MY HOME, I WOULD SEEK ASYLUM ELSEWHERE FASTER THAN YOU CAN SAY 'FAKE ID'.

FRENCH

Si ce pays était le mien, je demanderais l'asile ailleurs plus vite que tu peux dire «faux-papiers».

GERMAN

Wenn dieses Land mein Heimat wäre, würde ich schneller anderswo Asyl beantragen als du einen Ausweis verfälschen könntest.

ITALIAN

Se questo paese fosse il mio cercerei asilo altrove prima che tu abbia il tempo di dire «documenti falsi».

SPANISH

Si este país fuera mi casa, buscaría asilo en otro lugar antes que puedas decir «documento de identidad falso».

IF YOU COULD JUST LISTEN TO YOURSELF... THAT ACCENT OF YOURS IS RIDICULOUS.

FRENCH

*Si seulement tu pourrais t'entendre…
cet accent est tellement ridicule.*

GERMAN

*Hör dich doch an… dein
Akzent ist lächerlich.*

ITALIAN

*Se tu ti potessi sentire… Il tuo
accento è veramente ridicolo.*

SPANISH

*Si te escucharas… encontrarías
ridículo tu acento.*

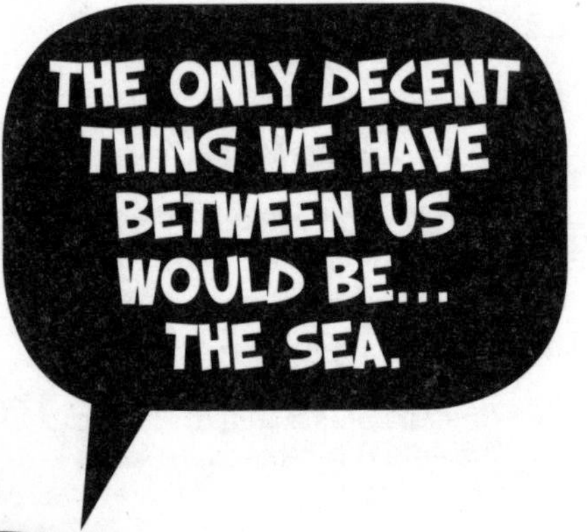
THE ONLY DECENT THING WE HAVE BETWEEN US WOULD BE... THE SEA.

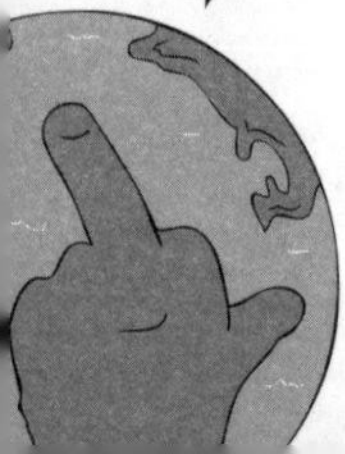

FRENCH

*La seule chose d'honorable qu'il
y a entre nous, c'est... la mer.*

GERMAN

*Die einzige gute Sache zwischen
uns wäre etwa… der Ärmelkanal.*

ITALIAN

*L'unica cosa che dovremmo
avere fra noi è... il mare.*

SPANISH

*La única cosa decente entre
tú y yo es… el mar.*

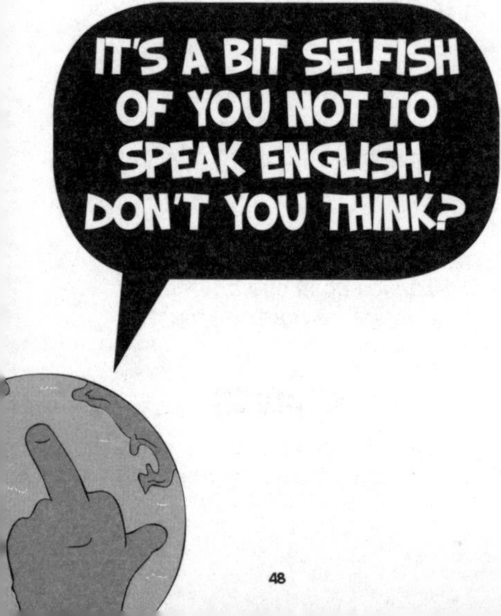
IT'S A BIT SELFISH OF YOU NOT TO SPEAK ENGLISH, DON'T YOU THINK?

FRENCH

C'est un peu égoïste de votre part de ne pas parler anglais, vous ne trouvez pas?

GERMAN

Es ist ziemlich unverschämt dass du kein Englisch sprichst, meinst du nicht?

ITALIAN

Non conoscere l'inglese è un po' egoista da parte tua, non credi?

SPANISH

Es egoísta por tu parte no hablar inglés. ¿No lo crees?

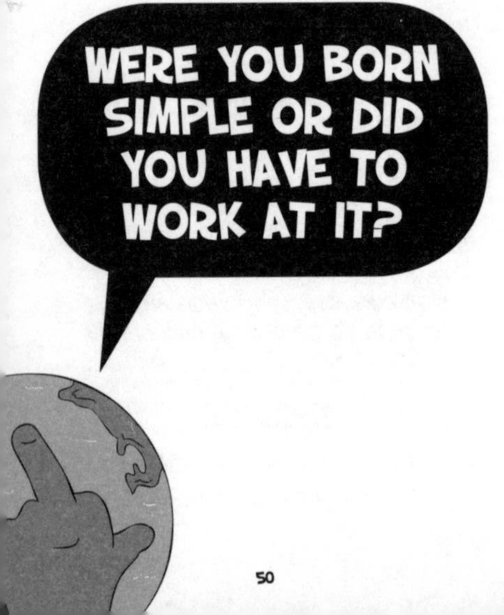
WERE YOU BORN SIMPLE OR DID YOU HAVE TO WORK AT IT?

FRENCH

Tu t'es né connard, ou t'as travaillé longtemps à l'atteindre?

GERMAN

Warst du als Idiot geboren oder müsstest du daran arbeiten?

ITALIAN

Sei nato stupido o ti sei impegnato per diventarlo?

SPANISH

¿Naciste poco inteligente o te costó mucho trabajo?

IT SMELLS LIKE I'VE GOT SOME SHIT STUCK TO MY SHOE - YES, IT'S YOUR COUNTRY.

FRENCH

Ça sent comme si j'ai de la merde collée sous la chaussure – bien oui, c'est votre pays.

GERMAN

Es stinkt so als ob ich Hundescheisse auf die Schuhe habe – ach ja, es hängt von eurem Land ab.

ITALIAN

Puzza come se avessi della merda attaccata alla scarpa – si, è il tuo paese.

SPANISH

Huele como lo tengo mierda pegada en el zapato – ah, es tu país.

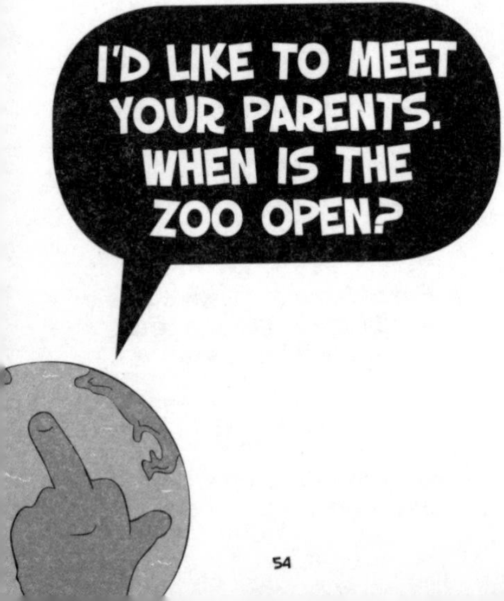
I'D LIKE TO MEET YOUR PARENTS. WHEN IS THE ZOO OPEN?

FRENCH

J'aimerais bien rencontrer tes parents. Tu connais les horaires d'ouverture du zoo?

GERMAN

Ich würde schon gerne deinen Eltern treffen. Wan hat der Zoo offen?

ITALIAN

Vorrei conoscere i tuoi genitori. Quando apre lo zoo?

SPANISH

Me gustaría conocer a tus padres. ¿Cuando esta el zoo abierto?

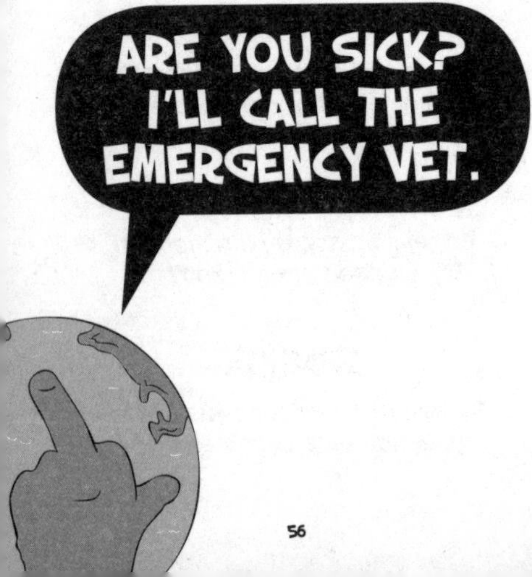
ARE YOU SICK? I'LL CALL THE EMERGENCY VET.

FRENCH

Tu es malade? Je vais appeler un vétérinaire d'urgence.

GERMAN

Bist du Krank? Ich ruf schon mal den Tierarzt.

ITALIAN

Ti senti male? Chiamo l'emergenza veterinaria.

SPANISH

¿Estás enfermo? Llamaré al veterinario.

FRENCH

*Si tu étais deux fois plus intelligent,
tu serais encore stupide.*

GERMAN

*Und wenn du doppelt so schlau
wärst, wärst du immer noch doof.*

ITALIAN

*Anche con il doppio della tua
intelligenza, saresti ancora stupido.*

SPANISH

*Si fueras el doble de inteligente,
aún serías estúpido.*

FOOD & DRINK

FRENCH

Servez-vous boissons avec des glaçons qui ne contiennent pas de matière fécale?

GERMAN

Servieren Sie Getränke mit Eis dass nicht von hintelassene Scheisse gemacht worden ist?

ITALIAN

Servite bibite con ghiaccio che non sia fatto di merda?

SPANISH

¿El hielo de las bebidas procede de depósitos fecales?

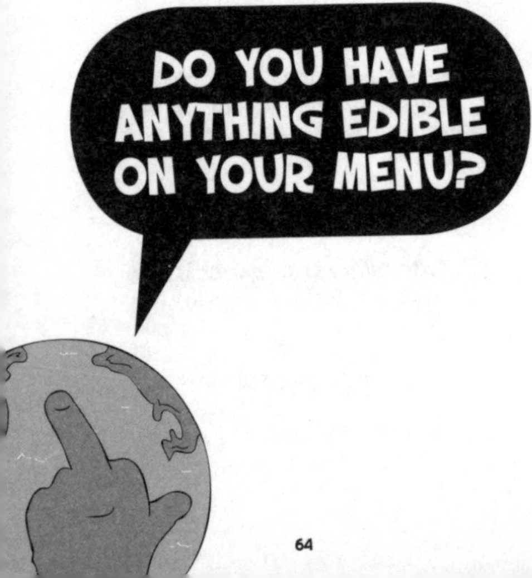
DO YOU HAVE ANYTHING EDIBLE ON YOUR MENU?

FOOD & DRINK

FRENCH

Votre menu a-t-il quelque chose de comestible?

GERMAN

Gibts etwas esbares auf Ihrem Menu?

ITALIAN

Avete niente di commestibile sul menu?

SPANISH

¿Tiene algo comestible en el menú?

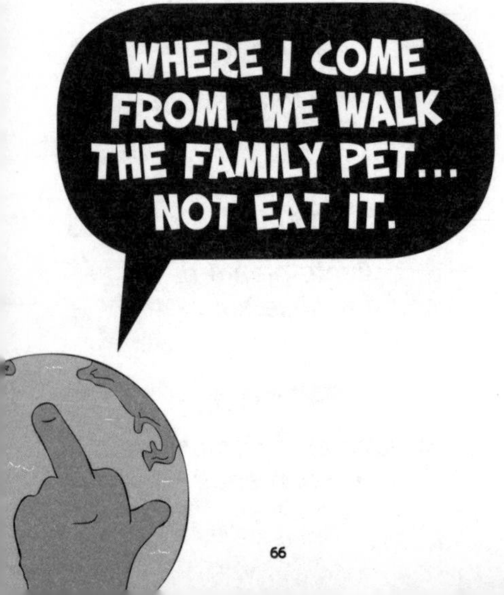
WHERE I COME FROM, WE WALK THE FAMILY PET... NOT EAT IT.

FRENCH

Chez moi, les animaux de compagnie on les promène, on ne les bouffe pas.

GERMAN

Bei uns nimmt man die Haustiere mit spazieren… nicht als Vorspeise.

ITALIAN

Nel mio paese gli animali domestici li portiamo a spasso, non li mangiamo.

SPANISH

De donde yo vengo, paseamos a las mascotas… no nos las comemos.

THANKS TO YOUR DISGUSTING LOCAL CUISINE, DIETING HAS NEVER BEEN SO EASY.

FRENCH

Grâce à votre cuisine de pays dégueulasse, faire un régime n'a jamais été aussi facile.

GERMAN

Dank Ihrer scheuslischen einheimische Küche, fiel mir das Abnehmen nie so leicht ein.

ITALIAN

Con la vostra cucina schifosa non è mai stato così facile stare a dieta.

SPANISH

Gracias por tu asquerosa cocina, nunca fue tan fácil ponerse a dieta.

HYGIENE

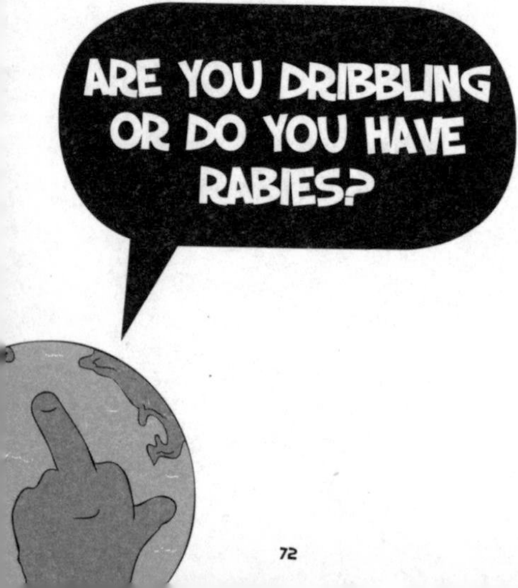
ARE YOU DRIBBLING OR DO YOU HAVE RABIES?

FRENCH

Baves-tu ou tu as la rage?

GERMAN

*Sabberst du oder
hast du Tollwut?*

ITALIAN

Stai sbavando o hai la rabbia?

SPANISH

¿Babeas o tienes la rabia?

I HAVE A LITTLE IRRITATION DOWN BELOW. AH YES, I SEE IT'S EUROPE. IN THAT CASE, THERE'S NO CURE.

FRENCH

J'ai une légére irritation à la base. Ah! Je vois, c'est l'Europe. Donc, il n'y a aucun remède.

GERMAN

Mir juckt's recht schlecht am Arsch. Ach ja, das wäre etwa Europa. Deshalb gibt's auch kein Heilmittel.

ITALIAN

Ho del prurito laggiù. Ah, è l'Europa. Beh, in questo caso non c'è rimedio.

SPANISH

Tengo algo irritante ahí abajo. ¡Ah! Ya veo. Es Europa. En ese caso, no tiene solución.

FRENCH

Je peux vous emprunter un tuyau d'arrosage? Votre pays a besoin d'un nettoyage de colon.

GERMAN

Kanst du mir mal 'nen Schlauch leihen? Dein Land hat 'ne Arschdurchspülung nötig.

ITALIAN

Hai un tubo da prestarmi? Il tuo paese ha bisogno di un'irrigazione anale.

SPANISH

¿Tienes alguna manguera que pueda tomar prestada? Tu país necesita ser regado por colonialistas.

SO THAT'S WHAT SYPHILIS LOOKS LIKE. ARE THERE ANY OTHER INDIGENOUS CONDITIONS THAT I SHOULD KNOW ABOUT?

FRENCH

*Voilà donc a quoi ressemble
la Syphilis. Y a t-il d'autres
affections indigenes que je
devrais connaître?*

GERMAN

*So sieht Syfilis aus. Gibt's weitere
einheimische Erkrankungen über
die ich mich informieren sollte?*

ITALIAN

*Quindi questa è la sifilide…
Ci sono altre malattie locali di
cui dovrei essere al corrente?*

SPANISH

*Así que eso es la sífilis. ¿Hay alguna
otra enfermedad que debo conocer?*

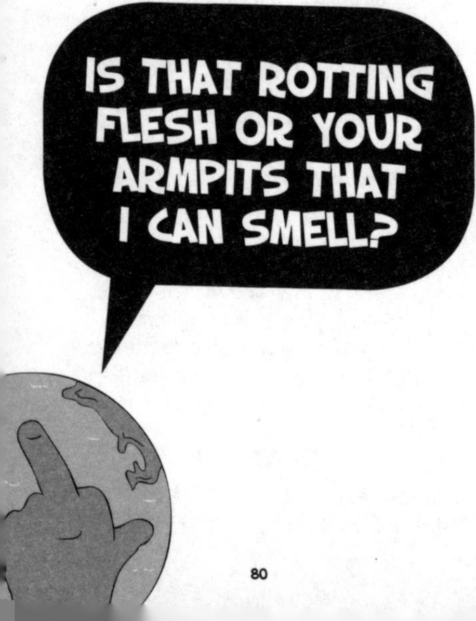
IS THAT ROTTING FLESH OR YOUR ARMPITS THAT I CAN SMELL?

FRENCH

*Est-ce de la viande avariée ou
tes aisselles, cette odeur?*

GERMAN

*Ist das verfaultes Fleisch oder deine
Unterarme die ich da rieche?*

ITALIAN

*E' odore di carne marcia o
sono le tue ascelle?*

SPANISH

*¿Huele a carne podrida
o son tus sobacos?*

WHY HAS NO ONE THOUGHT OF IMPORTING DEODORANTS TO YOUR COUNTRY?

FRENCH

Pourquoi personne n'a jamais pensé à importer du déodorant à votre pays?

GERMAN

Wieso hat man noch nie Deo in eurem Land eingeführt?

ITALIAN

Perché nessuno ha mai pensato di importare deodoranti nel tuo paese?

SPANISH

¿Por qué no se piensa en importar desodorantes a tu país?

FRENCH

On ne doit pas être très loin de la mer, ça sent le poisson. Oh! Pardon, on est dans le quartier des bordels.

GERMAN

Sind wir etwa an der Küste, es riecht nach Fisch. Ach so, hier gibt's lauter Bordellen.

ITALIAN

Dobbiamo essere vicini al mare, sento odore di pesce. Oh, è il vostro quartiere a luci rosse…

SPANISH

Debemos estar cerca del mar. Puedo oler a pescado. ¡Ah! Es el distrito de las putas.

FRENCH

Votre littoral a besoin d'un coup de propre. Une catastrophe naturelle d'envergure ferait l'affaire.

GERMAN

Ihre Küste ist ziemlich verschmutzt. Ein grossgelangeten Naturkatastrophe könnte schon als Reinigung reichen.

ITALIAN

La vostra costa ha bisogno di una pulita… un grande disastro naturale potrebbe essere la soluzione.

SPANISH

Vendría bien limpiar el litoral… un tremendo desastre natural podría hacerlo.

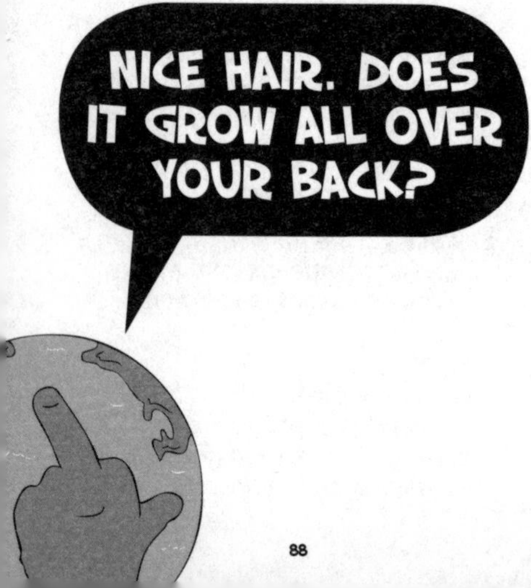
NICE HAIR. DOES IT GROW ALL OVER YOUR BACK?

FRENCH

Tu as les cheveaux très beaux. Ils pousent sur tout le dos également?

GERMAN

Schone Haare hast du. Wachsen sie am ganzen Rücken?

ITALIAN

Che bei capelli. Ti crescono su tutta la schiena?

SPANISH

Bonito pelo. ¿Lo tienes igual por todo el cuerpo?

TRANSPORT

FRENCH

J'ai passé une semaine au salon d'embarquement avant d'arriver enfin à votre pays. C'était la plus belle semaine des vacances.

GERMAN

Ich habe 'ne ganze Woche im Wartesaal beim Abflug verbracht. Das war die beste Woche meines Urlaubs.

ITALIAN

Ho passato una settimana nella sala di partenze prima di arrivare finalmente nel vostro paese. E' stata la migliore settimana della vacanza.

SPANISH

Espere una semana en la sala de embarque antes de llegar a tu país. Fue lo mejor de las vacaciones.

FRENCH

*Les trains chez nous
sentaient presque aussi
mauvais que les vôtres.*

GERMAN

*Unsere Bahnzüge stinken
fast so schlecht wie Eure.*

ITALIAN

*I nostri treni puzzano
quasi come i vostri.*

SPANISH

*Nuestros trenes olían tan
mal como los tuyos.*

FRENCH

On dirait que votre système de circulation a été créée par une équippe de singes retardés.

GERMAN

Euer Verkehrsnetzwerk ist wahrscheinlich von ein Gemeinschaft retardierten Affen hergestellt worden.

ITALIAN

Le vostre strade sembrano state disegnate da una squadra di scimmie ritardate.

SPANISH

Tu sistema de tráfico parece que estaba diseñado por un equipo de monos retrasados.

SEXUAL

FRENCH

Je suppose que de baiser entre frères et soeurs vous épargne opportunément les services d'une agence matrimoniale.

GERMAN

Ich vermute dass vor lauter sex innerhalb der Verwandschaft, sie Partner Treff oder Dating nicht nötig haben.

ITALIAN

Penso che far sesso con i tuoi parenti eviti la necessità di contattare agenzie matrimoniali.

SPANISH

Follar con tus hermanos hace innecesarias las agencias matrimoniales.

FRENCH

*Dans mon pays, il n'est pas
normal pour les femmes d'avoir
des poils à cet endroit.*

GERMAN

*In unserem Land haben Frauen in dem
Bereich normalerweise keine Haare.*

ITALIAN

*Nel mio paese non è normale
che le donne abbiano peli là.*

SPANISH

*En mi país, las mujeres no
suelen tener pelo en el coño.*

FRENCH

Grâce à toi, maintenant ça me brûle quand je pisse.

GERMAN

Du bist zu danken dafür das es beim pissen weh tut.

ITALIAN

Grazie a te, ora mi fa' male quando piscio.

SPANISH

Gracias a ti, ahora me duele cuando meo.

IF WE'RE GOING TO SLEEP TOGETHER I'M GOING TO HAVE TO INSIST WE DO IT IN THE DARK.

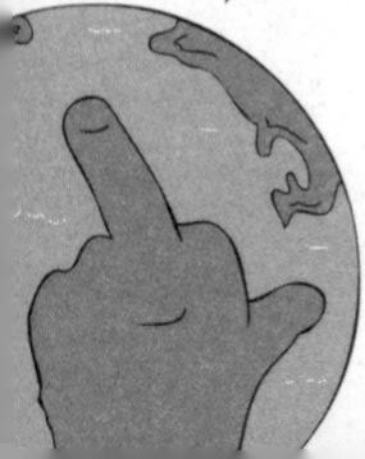

FRENCH

Si tu vas te coucher avec moi, il faut que j'insiste le faire dans le noir.

GERMAN

Wenn wir zusammen schlafen warden, muss ich darauf verlangen, dass wir es im dunklem machen.

ITALIAN

Se dobbiamo fare sesso devo insistere di farlo al buio.

SPANISH

Si vamos a follar tendré a insistir que hacemos sin las luces encendidas.

I SEEM TO HAVE COMPLETELY LOST MY SEX DRIVE SINCE VISITING YOUR COUNTRY.

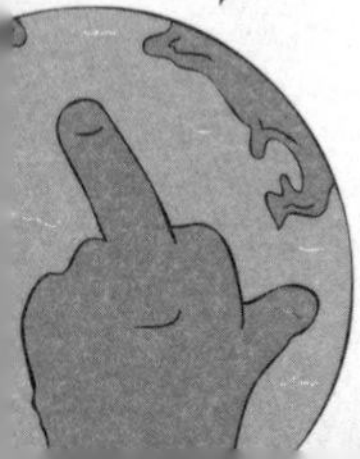

FRENCH

Il me semble que j'ai tout à fait perdu l'appétit sexuel depuis mon arrive dans ton pays.

GERMAN

Seit dem ich bei dir im Lande bin, bin ich gar nicht mehr an Sex interesert.

ITALIAN

Da quando sono nel tuo paese mi e' completamente passata la voglia di fare sesso.

SPANISH

He perdido completamente mi deseo de follar desde que visite tu país.

UGLY

YOU HAVE A GREAT FACE... FOR RADIO.

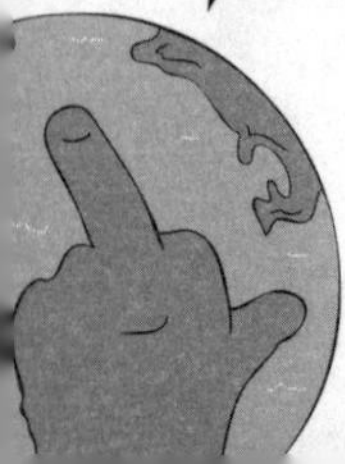

FRENCH

*T'as un visage magnifique…
pour faire de la radio.*

GERMAN

*Du hast ein tolles
Gesicht… für's Radio.*

ITALIAN

*Hai la faccia perfetta…
per la radio.*

SPANISH

*Tienes una bonita
cara… para la radio.*

I MAY BE DRUNK, BUT IN THE MORNING I'LL BE SOBER AND YOU'LL STILL BE UGLY.

FRENCH

Peut-être que j'ai trop bu, mais demain matin je ne serai plus ivre et tu serais toujours aussi moche.

GERMAN

Ich weiss nicht wie ich dich am besten beschreiben sollte. Gibt's da was stärkeres als hässlich?

ITALIAN

Lo sarò anche ubriaco, ma domani mattina io sarò sobrio e tu sarai sempre brutta.

SPANISH

Yo puedo estar borracho, pero por la mañana yo estaré sobrio y tu seguirás siendo feo.

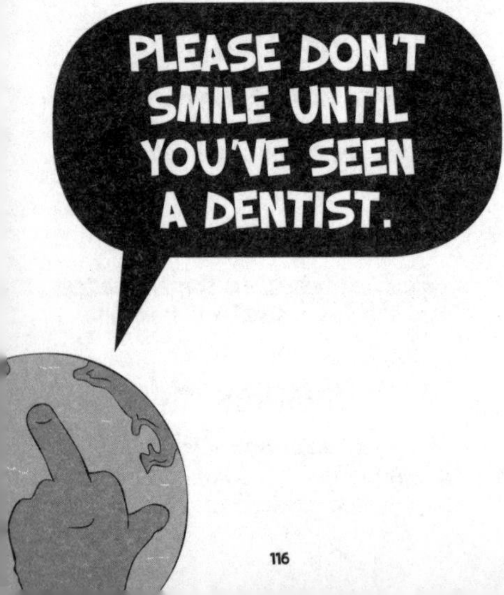
PLEASE DON'T SMILE UNTIL YOU'VE SEEN A DENTIST.

FRENCH

*S'il te plaît, ne souris pas
avant d'avoir vu un dentiste.*

GERMAN

*Lächele bitte nicht bevor
du beim Zahnarzt warst.*

ITALIAN

*Non sorridere se prima
non vai dal dentista.*

SPANISH

*Por favor, no sonrías hasta
haber visitado a un dentista.*

I THINK YOU'RE VERY BRAVE TO SHOW YOUR FACE IN PUBLIC WITHOUT A PAPER BAG TO COVER IT.

FRENCH

Je croix que tu as beaucoup de courage de te montrer en public sans mettre un sac sur la tête.

GERMAN

Du bist schon sehr mutig dich so in der Öffentlichkeit zeigen zu lassen ohne einen Sack auf dem Kopf zu tragen.

ITALIAN

Hai del coraggio a farti vedere in pubblico a volto scoperto.

SPANISH

Creo que eres muy valiente por mostrar tu cara en público sin una bolsa que la cubra.

RANDOM INSULTS
FROM AROUND THE WORLD

ARABIC

BOOS TEEZEE:
kiss my arse

CHARRA ALAIK:
shit on you

SHARMUTE:
bastard

KUL KHARA!:
eat shit!

HEBREW

LECH ZAYEN PARA:
go fuck a cow

BEN ZSONA:
son of a bitch

INAHL RABAK ARS YA CHOOSHARMUTA:
go to hell with your fucking father

STOM TA'PEH:
shut your cakehole

JAPANESE

BAKA:
stupid

BAKAYAROU:
arsehole

CHIPATAMA:
dickhead

KUSO SHITE SHINEZO:
die shitting

NORWEGIAN

MORAPULER:
motherfucker

FITTE:
cunt

KUK SUGER:
knobsucker

STOGGING:
face like the back of a bus

RUSSIAN

BL'AD:
bitch

GOVN'UK:
bastard

KURITE MOJU TRUBKU:
suck my cock

YEB VAS:
fuck off

WELSH

WYNEB CACH:
shit face

CONT TEW:
fat cunt

BWYTA FY GACHU:
eat my excretion

PIGYN BACH:
tiny cock

If you're interested in finding out more about our humour books, follow us on Twitter: @SummersdaleLOL

www.summersdale.com